101

Ways to Avoid

Spelling

Traps

101
Ways to Avoid
Spelling
Traps

by Linda Williams Aber

illustrated by Barbara Levy

For Kip

CONTENTS

Chapter 1

Spell Well . . .
and Lots of Other Words!

You may not believe this, but it's true: If the great English poet and playwright William Shakespeare were alive today, he would not pass a spelling test. Shakespeare didn't even bother to spell his own name the same way every time he wrote it. Chances are he wasn't concerned about spelling skills, because nobody else spelled well either! Back in those days—the sixteenth century—spelling rules had not yet been created.

So, if Shakespeare didn't care about spelling, why should you? The answer is *communication.*

If we did not all spell words the same way, we would have a very difficult time reading and understanding each other's writing. When we all write and spell by the same rules, life is easier. For example, imagine you are taking a walk. You come to a corner and see a sign that says QJMK. On the next corner another sign says ETGB. On the third corner a sign says STOP.

You'll know what to do at the third corner because you know what STOP means. Everyone who reads the English language knows what STOP means. Luckily, someone decided that STOP should always be spelled s-t-o-p. Thanks to that rule, we don't have to guess what the sign means. We know.

Spelling is important, but not everyone finds it easy to spell well. Memorizing how words are spelled is the best way to remember their correct spelling. Some people seem to be able to memorize the spelling of a word after looking at it just once. Other people might look at the word a hundred times but not remember how to spell it. Each of us, however, needs to discover a dependable way to remember how words are spelled. This book takes a close look at how words are created and offers tips and techniques for improving your spelling skills. Study them all and use the ones that work best for you. Along your way to becoming a better speller, have fun with the puzzles and word games. Answers to the puzzles begin on page 82.

Are you ready to spell well?

W - E - L - L

Great! Now, are you ready to spell some other words too? Start with good spelling habits. Remember: *Good spelling habits lead to good grades—and to better communication.*

Before you start, assemble a few spelling tools and learn some simple techniques for improving your spelling.

1. Get a good dictionary. There are many different dictionaries. Choose one that is easy to read and easy to use. Why strain your eyes trying to read tiny letters? Find one with type that is big enough to be seen by the human eye without the help of a magnifying glass! Ask your teacher to recommend a dictionary that is appropriate for your grade level.

2. Make a list of frequently misspelled words. Use pages 90–91 at the back of this book to keep a master list of words you often misspell. When you hear a new word, write the word on your list and learn it later.

3. Learn the four Standard Spelling Rules, which are explained in this book.

They are: The *I-E* Rule (page 19), The Double-Consonant Rule (page 48), The Final *Y* Rule (page 52), and The Final *E* Rule (page 53).

4. Pronounce the word. Look at the word and say it out loud. Listen closely to the way it sounds. Pronouncing a word incorrectly can make you misspell it. If you say sep-*er*-ate instead of sep-*a*-rate, you will probably spell the word incorrectly. Make sure you know how to pronounce the word. Then practice saying it.

5. Study the word. Examine the word the way you might examine something under a magnifying glass.

•Look at the whole word.
•Say the letters in order.
•Count the letters in the word.
•Divide the word into syllables. A syllable is a word part that can be pronounced by itself. For example, breaking the word *separate* into three shorter parts—*sep-a-rate*—can make the individual letters easier to remember.
•Study each part of the word. Pay special attention to any parts that might be tricky. Are there silent letters? Are there consonants that don't sound like you expect them to

sound? Are there any words inside the word? (For example, there is "a rat" in separate.)

•Make up memory tricks that will help you spell a particular word. To remember that there are two s's in the word *dessert,* for example, remind yourself that you would like a second serving of dessert.

Take time out to practice with this word-in-a-word puzzle. Find the word hidden in the last word of each line. Underline each word in a word. (The first one is done for you.) You'll soon see that spelling can be fun—and funny!

Find a cap in CHAT,

A musician in BACHELOR,

Some blubber in FATALISTIC,

And a vegetable in PEACEMAKER.

There's a small bed in MASCOT,

And a little rug in CHECKMATE.

Find a saucepan in COMPOTE,

And the end in BALLAST.

6. Write the word. The more you write, the better you will be at spelling. Write the word while looking at it. Then cover the word and write it from memory. As you try to remember how to spell the word, recall what you learned from studying it—how many letters it has, whether it has a silent letter or a double consonant or a word within the word.

7. Use your dictionary. If you aren't sure how to spell a word, find it in a dictionary. Check the correct spelling and write it again from memory. If you have trouble finding words in a dictionary, keep an alphabet strip handy. Just print the alphabet across the top of a sheet of paper. It will help you see the sequence of letters in the alphabet. Then you'll be able to figure out where a word might appear in the dictionary.

A B C D E F G H I J K L M N O P Q R S T U V W X Y Z

8. Check the meaning of the word. Knowing the definition of a word is even more important than knowing how to spell it, and sometimes the definition can help remind you of the spelling. Each time you use a word correctly in a sentence, you build your vocabulary. A good vocabulary will enrich your writing and your conversation and will make you more comfortable with all aspects of words, including spelling.

9. Use letter blocks and "touch" the word. Some people have an easier time learning to spell words if they use letter tiles or cubes, such as those found in the games Scrabble or Spill and Spell. If you can't memorize a word just by looking at it, try forming the word with letter blocks. The physical act of putting each letter of a word in its correct order can help you remember the spelling when you have to write the word.

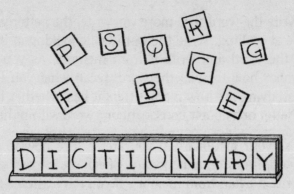

10. Start a spelling notebook. Keeping a notebook can be fun and helpful. Allow two or three pages for each letter of the alphabet. When you find a new word you are having trouble spelling:

•Write it under the correct letter in your notebook. Spell it correctly.
•Write the word again and circle the part of the word that gives you trouble.
•Write the definition of the word.
•Write a sentence using the word. Your sentences can be as serious or silly as you like. After all, it's your notebook!

Here's how one entry in your spelling notebook might look:

A a

Word: answer   ans(wer)

Definition: reply

Sentence: When the teacher asked me to spell the word answer, I did not answer.

14

Hint: Learning how to spell one word might help you spell some related words. The related words may be formed by adding prefixes, suffixes, or other endings. For example, if you can spell *place,* you probably can spell *replace, placed,* and *replacement.*

Write three words that are related to the word *view.*

1. _____   2. _____   3. _____

11. Think about all the words you already know. Do you think you can't spell? You might be surprised at how well you spell already. Here are the 56 words that are most often used in writing. They are listed in order of how often they are used.

Have a friend test you on these words to find out how many of them you can already spell correctly. Give yourself two points for each word you spell right!

the, of, and, a, to, in, is, you, that, it, he, for, was, on, are, as, with, his, they, at, be, this, from, I, have, or, by, one, had, not, but, what, each, about, how, up, out, them, then, she, many, some, so, these, would, other, into, has, more, her, words, called, just, where, most, know

See? You probably got a very good score on this test. That means you are already able to spell the words most often used in writing. Spelling well is fun. Keep going!

Chapter 2

Vowel Sounds:
The Long and Short of It

12. Spelling is easier if you take the word apart sound by sound rather than trying to spell the whole word at once.

Start with vowel sounds. Vowel sounds may be long or short. Vowel sounds can be made two different ways: either by the vowel letters —*A, E, I, O, U,* and sometimes *Y*—alone or by combining them with other letters. Learning how the different vowel sounds are spelled is a good way to strengthen your spelling skills.

13. The Long *A* sound may be spelled *a, ai, ay,* or *a*-consonant-*e* (such as *ane*).

The words in Column 1 have the Long *A* sound. Say the words aloud and listen for the Long *A* sound. In Column 2 write two words that rhyme with each word in Column 1 and have the same letter patterns.

Column 1	Column 2	
1. able	_____	_____
2. afraid	_____	_____
3. pay	_____	_____
4. lane	_____	_____

14. The Long *E* sound may be spelled *e, ee, ea, e*-consonant-*e* (such as *ede*), or *ie.*

The words in Column 1 have the Long *E* sound. Say the words aloud and listen for the Long *E* sound. In Column 2 write two words that rhyme with each word in Column 1 and have the same letter patterns.

Column 1	Column 2	
1. me	_____	_____
2. weed	_____	_____
3. team	_____	_____
4. recede	_____	_____
5. brief	_____	_____

Hint: When you add *e* to the end of a word, the vowel sound may change from short to long. For example:

man/mane   din/dine   can/cane   met/mete   hop/hope
cap/cape   cub/cube   tap/tape   hat/hate

15. RULE ALERT! RULE ALERT! Here is the first of the four rules you need to know to spell well.

Standard Spelling Rule #1: The *I-E* Rule

This rule, which happens to rhyme, will help you remember how to spell words in which *ie* makes the Long *E* sound:

> *i* before *e*
> Except after *c*
> Or when sounded as *a*
> As in *neighbor* or *weigh*.

Here are some examples of words that follow the rules in the rhyme.

achieve	chief	niece	shield	ceiling*
believe	field	piece	thief	deceit*
brief	grief	relief	yield	receive*

* Notice in these three words the Long *E* sound is spelled *ei* because it comes after the letter *c*.

Practice spelling words that have the Long *E* sound and include either *ie* or *ei*. Write *ie* or *ei* to complete the following words:

1. bel__ __ve   4. rec__ __ve   7. hyg__ __ne

2. dec__ __t   5. gr__ __f   8. retr__ __ve

3. p__ __ce   6. rel__ __f

Practice spelling *ie* words that have the Long *A* sound. Fill in the spaces with the missing letters *ei*.

1. n__ __ghbor   3. w__ __ght

2. r__ __ndeer   4. sl__ __gh

Hint: The following words are exceptions to the *I-E* Rule:

either neither seize weird leisure financier species

Here's a sentence to help you remember these exceptions:

At his leisure, neither financier would seize either weird species.

16. Here are some fun facts about the Long *E* sound in words ending with *-cede, -ceed,* and *-sede:*

In the English language, only one word ends in *-sede.* That word is *supersede.* Only three words end in *-ceed.* Those words are *exceed, proceed,* and *succeed.* All other words with this sound end in *-cede.*

20

17. The Long *I* sound may be spelled *i, y, igh,* or *i*-consonant-*e* (such as *ine*).

The words in Column 1 have the Long *I* sound. Say the words aloud and listen for the Long *I* sound. In Column 2 write two words that rhyme with each word in Column 1 and have the same letter patterns.

Column 1   Column 2

1. find   _____   _____
2. shy   _____   _____
3. high   _____   _____
4. shine   _____   _____

18. The Long *O* sound may be spelled *o, oa, ough,* or *o*-consonant-*e* (such as *ode*).

The words in Column 1 have the Long *O* sound. Say the words aloud and listen for the Long *O* sound. In Column 2 write two words that rhyme with each word in Column 1 and have the same letter patterns.

Column 1   Column 2

1. go   _____   _____
2. goat   _____   _____
3. dough   _____   _____
4. code   _____   _____

19. *U* is an unusual vowel. The Long *U* has the *YU* sound as in *cube* and *use*. These sounds may be spelled *u, ew, ui,* or *u*-consonant-*e* (such as *une*). Some people say the *OO* sound in *rule* and *July* is also the Long U sound. This sound may also be spelled *oo*.

The words in Column 1 have the *YU* sound or the *OO* sound. Say the words aloud and listen for the *YU* or *OO* sound. In Column 2 write two words that rhyme with each word in Column 1 and have the same letter patterns.

Column 1   Column 2

1. cue   _____   _____

2. few   _____   _____

3. suit   _____   _____

4. tune   _____   _____

5. moon   _____   _____

20. Short vowel sounds are usually spelled with the single vowel letter.

Short *a* may be spelled *a*.

Short *e* may be spelled *e*.

Short *i* may be spelled *i*.

Short *o* may be spelled *o*.

Short *u* may be spelled *u*.

Three examples of each short vowel sound are listed below. Say the sample words aloud. Listen for the short vowel sound in each word. Then, in the word list that follows, find the words that have short vowel sounds.

Short *a* sound—bat, flag, chatter
   Circle the words that have the Short *a* sound:
   cage   bad   factory   manners   name   catch

Short *e* sound—pet, sense, stretch
   Circle the words that have the Short *e* sound:
   seven   mess   keep   team   dent   helmet

Short *i* sound—ship, witch, pin
   Circle the words that have the Short *i* sound:
   find   fish   mint   spider   into   picnic

Short *o* sound—pond, clock, sock
   Circle the words that have the Short *o* sound:
   pot   locket   code   tongs   movie   bother

Short *u* sound—hundred, shut, punch
   Circle the words that have the Short *u* sound:
   nut   bundle   tune   fruit   hurry   but

21. Practice what you've learned about words that have short vowel sounds.

Choose a word from the following list that matches one of the ten definitions shown below. Write the word in the space provided, and then circle the letter in that word that has a short vowel sound. Fill in all ten blanks.

band	tent	spaceship	shopkeeper	hunt
cap	west	pitch	stop	sun

1. astronaut's vehicle _____

2. sky light _____

3. music group _____

4. store owner _____

5. search _____

6. camping house _____

7. opposite of go _____

8. hat _____

9. throw _____

10. opposite of east _____

22. Practice what you've learned about spelling words that have long vowel sounds.

Choose a word from the following list that belongs in one of the ten word groups shown below. Write the word in the space provided, and then circle the letter or letters in that word that have the long vowel sound. Fill in all ten blanks.

grapefruit	sleet	nine	toe	ukulele
lake	team	pine	boat	tune

1. heel, ankle, _____

2. song, melody, _____

3. seven, eight, _____

4. wind, rain, _____

5. elm, oak, _____

6. train, plane, _____

7. sport, players, _____

8. river, pond, _____

9. orange, lemon, _____

10. guitar, banjo, _____

dge sounds like *j*
ph sounds like *f*
kn sounds like *n*
wr sounds like *r*

Chapter 3

Consonant Sounds and Other Sounds

23. Consonants are all the letters of the alphabet except for the vowels: B, C, D, F, G, H, J, K, L, M, N, P, Q, R, S, T, V, W, X, Y, Z.

24. Most of the time, consonant sounds are spelled by individual consonant letters. A consonant sound may also be spelled by a combination of consonant letters. (For example, the sound *k* is spelled *ck* in the word *trick*.) Sometimes when consonant letters are combined, they spell the sound of a different letter.

The consonants shown in Column 1 can be used to spell the sounds shown in Column 2.

Column 1		Column 2
ss, sc, ce, c, ci, si, ssi, ti	⟷	s
ph, gh	⟷	f
gh, gu, gue	⟷	g
dge, g, di, ge	⟷	j
que, c, ck, ch, che, q	⟷	k

ll, el, tle, le	←————————→	l
gn, kn, pn	←————————→	n
wr, rh	←————————→	r
s, se, z, zz, x	←————————→	z

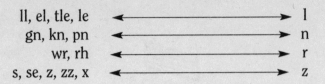

25. The consonant *c* can make an *s* sound or a *k* sound. Read the words listed below. Then, next to each word, write "s" for the *s* sound or "k" for the *k* sound.

1. cent_____ 7. color _____ 13. cut _____

2. candle _____ 8. cellar _____ 14. corner _____

3. pace_____ 9. climate_____ 15. city_____

4. cake_____ 10. citizen _____ 16. current _____

5. cereal _____ 11. cry _____ 17. cast _____

6. ceiling_____ 12. century ____ 18. deceit _____

Psst!
Here's a hint to help you pronounce these words. Notice that when e or i follows c, the c sounds like s. When a, o, u, l, or r follows c, the c sounds like k.

26. The consonant sound *f* may be spelled *f, gh,* or *ph.* Here's a phunny . . . oops! . . . funny poem for you to read. Circle the *f, gh,* or *ph* spelling mistakes as you find them.

Philip was a phrog,
Who croaked phrom noon to night.
The other frogs thought Filip
Was a very phunny sight.

CROAK!

A phrog named Phred called Philip
On the fone and said,
"Enouf! Your croaking's giving me
An aching in my head!"

"So sorry, Fred," said Philip.
"I meant not to ophend.
Phrom now on my croaking days
Have come to a phinal end!"

27. The consonant sound *g* may be spelled *g, gh, gu, or gue.* Read the following paragraph and circle the correctly spelled *g*-sound word in each set of parentheses.

On Halloween I was (aghast, agast) when I saw a (gost, ghost, goast) in a white (ghown, gown) eating (spagetti, spaghetti). I (guess, gess) I let down my (gard, guard) when he picked up a (gitar, guitar) and played a (vaguely, vagely) familiar tune.

28. At the beginning of a word, the consonant sound *j* may be spelled with the consonant letter *j* or the consonant letter *g* plus the vowel letter *e*. For example: jury, January, gem, general, geography.

29. At the end of a word, the *j* sound can be spelled *ge* or *dge*. The *ge* combination is used after a consonant, after a long vowel sound, and after two vowels. For example: *range, cage, Scrooge*. The *dge* combination is used at the end of a word or syllable directly after a single short vowel. For example: *badge, ledge*.

Use the above rules to determine how many words in the following list are spelled correctly. Write *T,* for *true,* if a word is spelled correctly. Write *F,* for *false,* if it's spelled incorrectly.

1. huge _____

2. brige _____

3. strange _____

4. age_____

5. juge _____

6. stage _____

7. sponge _____

8. plege _____

9. rige _____

10. knowledge_____

11. page_____

12. change _____

30. It does not happen often, but sometimes the consonant sound *k* may be spelled *que*. For example: *antique, technique*.

31. The *l* sound may be spelled *l, ll, el, tle,* and *le*. Use the clues in Column 1 to figure out the words in Column 2. Write the correct *l* sound combination to finish the words in Column 2.

Column 1	Column 2
small	litt _____
a grain of corn	kern _____
opposite of short	_____ ong
blow air through your teeth	whis _____
opposite of big	sma _____
whistles when water inside it boils	kett _____
a pair of pants has two	_____ egs
you can climb this	hi _____
you can blow these	bubb _____ s

32. The consonant sound *n* may be spelled *n, kn, gn,* or *pn.* Read the following paragraph and circle all the words that begin with the *n* sound.

> When Nellie was nine, she was knee-high to a grasshopper. She was the nicest girl in the neighborhood. One day Nellie knocked on my door and said she knew where a gnome was hiding! She had just seen one gnawing on a carrot. I know gnomes aren't real, but Nellie said this one was named Noah. I told her to come inside before the gnats got in and we both caught pneumonia!

33. The consonant sound *r* may be spelled *r, wr, or rh.* Can you tell write from right? Read the definitions on the next page and fill in the blanks with matching words from the word group in the box.

wrap rhombus rake rap wrist rain wrestling wrong ring

1. Not correct _____

2. Garden tool_____

3. Falling water_____

4. Cover a gift _____

5. Wear a watch here _____

6. Popular style of music _____

7. Sport _____

8. Bell sound_____

9. A parallelogram with four equal sides _____

34. The consonant sound *z* may be spelled *s, se, z, zz,* or *x*. Notice how the *z* sound is spelled in Column 1. Using that spelling, write another word with the *z* sound in Column 2.

	Column 1	Column 2
z sound spelled *s*:	has	_____
z sound spelled *se*:	tease	_____
z sound spelled *z*:	Oz	_____
z sound spelled *zz*:	buzz	_____
z sound spelled *x*:	xylophone	_____

35. Learn when to use the spelling *-ought* or *-aught*. As you read the following story, fill in the blanks with either *-ought* or *-aught*. Then check the answers at the back of the book to see if all of your answers are correct.

MY MOST EMBARRASSING MOMENT

It was my first day at my new school. I was sitting in the school cafeteria at lunchtime. I had br_____ my lunch from home. I opened my lunch bag and took out my salami sandwich. Then I went to the counter and b_____ a carton of milk. I came back to the table, sat down, and took a bite out of my sandwich. Suddenly, the girl next to me screamed out h_____ily, "Hey! I just c_____ this new kid eating my salami sandwich!"

She grabbed the sandwich from me. I grabbed it back. I th_____ it was my sandwich. We f_____ over the sandwich until it was nothing more than crumbs. Soon the teacher came over to us. She grabbed me by the collar and said, "You are a n_____y girl! Why did you take my d_____er's sandwich? At this school we try to be more th_____ful toward each other."

I said I was sorry, which I was. I never th_____ I'd get c_____ eating someone else's salami sandwich. I don't even like salami! This experience t_____ me a good lesson: Each student _____ to eat the lunch he or she br_____!

There are no shortcuts to learn when *-ought* and *-aught* should be used. You will have to memorize the spellings of these words. If you're not sure how to spell a particular word, check the dictionary.

36. The letters *-ough* make different sounds.

-ough (o)

-ough (oo)

-ough (uf)

-ough (ow)

-ough (off)

Say each of the following words aloud. Write the correct sound (*o, oo, uf, ow,* or *off*) next to each word.

1. enough _____   2. cough _____   3. plough _____

4. though _____   5. rough _____   6. bough _____

7. tough _____   8. through _____

bicycle

unicycle

tricycle

Chapter 4

Prefixes Are
Just the Beginning!

37. A prefix is a syllable added to the beginning of a base word. When a prefix is added, it changes the meaning of the word.

38. A base word is a word that can stand alone. It is the part of the word that contains the basic meaning.

In this example, the base word is *connect*. The other words are formed by adding a beginning, which is called a prefix.

connect

disconnect

reconnect

39.
The meaning of the prefix is a clue to the meaning of the word. The following chart shows a list of prefixes, their meanings, and examples of words including the prefixes.

Prefix	Meaning	Example
ab-	away	abnormal
bi-	two	bicycle
con-	with	conjoin
dis-	not	disrespect
il-	not	illegal
im-	not	imperfect
in-	into	insight
in-	not	inoperable
ir-	not	irresponsible
mis-	wrong	misbehave
non-	not	nonsense
post-	after	postgame
pre-	before	preview
re-	again	review
re-	back	replace
sub-	under	submarine
super-	over; above	superclean
trans-	across	transatlantic
tri-	three	tricycle
un-	not	uneven
uni-	one	unicycle

40. Remember this important fact about prefixes: When you add a prefix to a base word, the spelling of the base word stays the same.

Now that you know this, you'll never misspell the word *misspell*!

41. Make a chart to help you remember this rule. Here are some prefixes added to base words to create new words:

Prefix	+	Base Word	=	New Word
dis-	+	satisfied	=	dissatisfied
in-	+	formal	=	informal
im-	+	proper	=	improper
un-	+	lucky	=	unlucky
pre-	+	heat	=	preheat
mis-	+	inform	=	misinform
re-	+	dial	=	redial
sub-	+	urban	=	suburban

Find the base words in the following list. Write each base word in the blank provided.

1. renew _____   6. unable _____

2. nonstop _____   7. discontinue _____

3. irregular _____   8. impossible _____

4. insane _____   9. illiterate _____

5. mislead _____   10. predate _____

42. One meaning of the prefix *in-* is "not." It changes the meaning of a word to its opposite, or negative. Create the negative of the following words by rewriting each with *in-* added to the beginning.

adequate _____   sincere _____

direct _____   expensive _____

appropriate _____   decisive _____

43. The prefix *in-* changes to *im-* before words that begin with the letters *m* and *p*.

Create the negative of the following words that begin with *m* and *p* by rewriting each with *im-* added to the beginning.

partial _____   patient _____

possible _____   probable _____

practical _____   precise _____

mature _____   modest _____

mobile _____   mortal _____

44. The prefix *un-* also means "not" and forms the negative meaning of a word.

Create the negative of the following words by rewriting each with *un-* added to the beginning.

happy _____   interested _____

used _____   opened _____

healthy _____   fair _____

45. Don't make the common *mis-* mistake! Remember the prefix rule: When you add a prefix to a word, the spelling of the base word stays the same. Notice what happens when you add the prefix *mis-* to the following words:

_____state   _____spell   _____step   _____spend

46. One meaning of the prefix *re-* is "again." For each definition in the following list, write a matching word in the blank provided. Use the definitions to give you clues, and remember, the prefix *re-* means "again."

1. To arrange again: _____

2. To construct again:_____

3. To make fresh again: _____

4. To put into the cycle again: _____

5. To capture again: _____

47. Practice your prefix skills in this match-up challenge. Draw a line to match each prefix in Column 1 with a word in Column 2.

Column 1	Column 2
pre-	happy
dis-	form
un-	assign
in-	heat
im-	satisfaction
con-	expensive
re-	proper

41

48. Use prefixes to help you figure out the meaning of a word. Look at the prefix of each underlined word in the following sentences and think about how the word is used. In the space provided, write what the underlined word means.

1. No one could read her writing; her writing was <u>illegible</u>.

_____

2. I did not finish my homework; my homework was <u>incomplete</u>.

_____

3. She asked for more juice; she wanted to <u>refill</u> her glass.

_____

4. Michael Jordan is the best basketball player; he is a <u>superathlete</u>.

_____

49. Don't be fooled by words that look as if they have prefixes but really do not. Here's a way to test if a word has a prefix: Say the meaning of the prefix along with the rest of the word. If it makes sense, it is a prefix. If it does not make sense, it is part of the base word. For example: the re- in *region* is part of the base word. Since "again gion" does not make sense, the re- in *region* is not a prefix.

Give the following words the prefix test. Some of them have prefixes, and others do not. Underline the prefixes as you find them.

1. superior   2. react   3. submarine   4. constant

5. review   6. union   7. collect   8. prepay

50. Practice your prefixes by taking "pop quizzes." Ask a friend or parent to make up short quizzes for you like the example below.

The six words with prefixes listed in the box are hidden in the sentences below. Underline them as you find them. The first one is done for you. Look for:

informal improper unlucky redial misinform dissatisfied

1. When the light turns <u>red I a</u>lways stop.

2. If we see the sun, lucky days are ahead for us.

3. Jim is in Form Four at the private boys' school.

4. My dad is satisfied with my report card grades.

5. The limp rope reached all the way down to the ground.

6. The teacher has had it in for Mallory ever since she fell asleep in school.

tall   tall<u>er</u>   tall<u>est</u>

Chapter 5

Suffixes Are
Just the Ending!

51. A suffix is a syllable added to the end of a word. When a suffix is added, it changes the meaning of the word.

52. The meaning of the suffix is a clue to the meaning of the word. This chart shows some suffixes, their meanings, and examples of words including the suffixes.

Suffix	Meaning	Example
-able	can be; able to be	breakable
-ation	action or process of	presentation
-ed	already happened	walked
-er	more	sharper
-er	one that does	baker
-est	most	fastest
-ful	full of	hopeful
-hood	condition of	boyhood
-ing	action or process of	sleeping
-ish	characteristic of	boyish

Suffix	Meaning	Example
-less	without	hopeless
-ly	in a way	happily
-ment	condition of	enjoyment
-ness	condition of	happiness
-ous	full of	glorious
-ship	state or condition of	friendship
-ward	in the direction of	backward

53. The suffixes *-less* and *-ful* often form adjectives, which are words that describe other words. For example: *Home* is a noun (a person, place, or thing). *Home + -less = homeless*, which is an adjective. Change the nouns in the word group below to adjectives by adding *-less* or *-ful*. Write the new word on the line.

Base Word (Noun)	+	Suffix (-less or -ful)	=	New Word (Adjective)
1. spot	+	-less	=	_____
2. care	+	-ful	=	_____
3. child	+	-less	=	_____
4. pain	+	-ful	=	_____
5. friend	+	-less	=	_____
6. mind	+	-ful	=	_____

54. The suffixes *-ment* and *-ness* often turn base words into nouns. For example: *Settle* is a verb (action word). *Settle + -ment = settlement,* which is a noun. Foolish is an adjective. *Foolish + -ness = foolishness,* also a noun.

Underline the suffix in each word below. Then write the base word on the line.

1. encouragement: _____

2. tenderness: _____

3. happiness: _____

4. engagement: _____

5. softness: _____

6. battlement: _____

55. Sometimes when a suffix is added to a base word, a letter at the end of the base word may be changed, dropped, or doubled.

For example: silly + -est = silliest (The *y* changes to *i*.)
              elope + -ing = eloping (An *e* is dropped.)
              win + -er = winner (The *n* is doubled.)

Change the following base words by adding suffixes. Write the new words in the blanks provided.

Base Word	+	Suffix	=	New Word
1. hairy	+	-er	=	_____
2. sunny	+	-est	=	_____
3. lovely	+	-er	=	_____
4. decode	+	-ing	=	_____
5. erode	+	-ed	=	_____
6. invade	+	-er	=	_____
7. thin	+	-est	=	_____
8. tan	+	-ing	=	_____
9. adore	+	-able	=	_____
10. victory	+	-ous	=	_____

56. RULE ALERT! RULE ALERT! Here is the second of the four rules you need to know to spell well.

(Read carefully! This one sounds very complicated, but it's worth learning because it will keep you from making a lot of spelling errors!) Ready?

Standard Spelling Rule #2: The Double-Consonant Rule

Before adding *-able, -ed, -er, -est, -ing, -ish,* or *-ous,* double the final consonant when the word meets one of the following conditions:

one-syllable word + suffix beginning with vowel
For example:
chop + *-ing* = chopping (double consonant)
snob + *-ish* = snobbish (double consonant)
beg + *-ed* = begged (double consonant)

two-syllable word with accent on last syllable + suffix beginning with vowel
For example:
begin + *-ing* = beginning (double consonant)
regret + *-able* = regrettable (double consonant)

Test yourself on the following one-syllable words. Should you double the final consonant? On the line next to each one-syllable word, finish spelling the word by adding the suffix *-ing*.

1. cram_____

2. grip_____

3. stab_____

Test yourself on the following two-syllable words having the accent on the last syllable. Should you double the final consonant? On the line next to each two-syllable word, finish spelling the word by adding the suffix *-ed*.

1. control _____

2. admit _____

3. equip _____

Test yourself on words that do not have the accent on the last syllable. Should you double the final consonant? On the line next to each two-syllable word, finish spelling the word by adding the suffix *-er*.

1. island _____

2. polish _____

3. custom _____

Practice the double-consonant rule here. Add *-able, -ed, -er, -est,* or *-ing* to the base words listed. Write the new word on the line provided. The first one is done for you.

One-Syllable Base Word	+	Suffix Beginning with a Vowel	=	New Word with Double Consonant
1. drop	+	-ing	=	dropping
2. quit	+	-er	=	_____
3. rob	+	-ed	=	_____
4. mad	+	-est	=	_____
5. stop	+	-able	=	_____
6. step	+	-ing	=	_____

Hint: The double-consonant rule does not apply to suffixes that begin with a consonant: commitment, sadness, mouthful, gladly.

57. When you add the suffix -*ly* to a word ending with *l*, keep both *l*'s.

For example:

Base Word	+	Suffix	=	New Word
real	+	-ly	=	really
actual	+	-ly	=	actually
usual	+	-ly	=	usually
formal	+	-ly	=	formally
casually	+	-ly	=	casually

58. When you add the suffix -*ness* to a word ending with *n*, keep both *n*'s.

For example:

Base Word	+	Suffix	=	New Word
open	+	-ness	=	openness
sudden	+	-ness	=	suddenness
mean	+	-ness	=	meanness
even	+	-ness	=	evenness
common	+	-ness	=	commonness

59. When adding a suffix that begins with a vowel to a one-syllable word that ends in a single consonant preceded by a single vowel, double the last consonant in the base word.

For example:

Base Word	+	Suffix	=	New Word
bat	+	-ing	=	batting
cut	+	-er	=	cutter
flag	+	-ed	=	flagged
pig	+	-ish	=	piggish

60.
When you add a suffix that begins with a vowel to a base word having two vowels in a row (for example: tr*ai*n, p*ee*l, d*ea*l, c*oo*l), do not double the consonant.

Practice the two-vowel base word rule. Add *-able, -ed, -er, -est, -ing, -ish,* or *-ous* after the base word. Write the new word on the line provided. The first one is done for you.

Two-Vowel Base Word	+	Suffix Beginning with a Vowel	=	New Word
1. train	+	-ing	=	training
2. teach	+	-er	=	_____
3. clean	+	-est	=	_____
4. fool	+	-ish	=	_____
5. weed	+	-ed	=	_____
6. fuel	+	-ing	=	_____
7. bear	+	-able	=	_____
8. riot	+	-ous	=	_____

One exception to this rule is the word *quit.* The final *t* is doubled when a suffix is added.

61. RULE ALERT! RULE ALERT! Here is the third of the four rules you need to know to spell well.

Standard Spelling Rule #3: The Final *Y* Rule

> When you add a suffix to a base word that ends with *y* following a consonant, you usually change the *y* to *i*. When you add a suffix to a word that ends with *y* following a vowel, you usually keep the *y*.

Examples of changing the *y* to *i:*

Base Word	+	Suffix	=	New Word
angry	+	-ly	=	angrily
busy	+	-ly	=	busily
fury	+	-ous	=	furious
happy	+	-ness	=	happiness
merry	+	-ment	=	merriment

Examples of keeping the *y:*

Base Word	+	Suffix	=	New Word
play	+	-ing	=	playing
destroy	+	-ed	=	destroyed
buy	+	-er	=	buyer

Here are two exceptions to the Final *Y* Rule: *say* becomes *said* and *pay* becomes *paid*.

62. RULE ALERT! RULE ALERT! Here is the fourth of the four rules you need to know to spell well.

Standard Spelling Rule #4: The Final *E* Rule

> When you add a suffix that begins with a vowel to a base word that ends in silent *e*, you usually drop the last *e* from the base word. When you add a suffix that begins with a consonant to a base word that ends in silent *e*, you usually keep the final *e*.

For example:

Base Word	+	Suffix	=	New Word
have	+	-ing	=	having
fame	+	-ous	=	famous
assure	+	-ed	=	assured
move	+	-ment	=	movement
home	+	-ward	=	homeward

Put the following base words and suffixes together:

1. care	+	-ing	=	_____
2. agree	+	-ment	=	_____
3. hope	+	-ful	=	_____
4. lone	+	-er	=	_____
5. free	+	-dom	=	_____
6. nine	+	-ty	=	_____
7. white	+	-est	=	_____
8. purple	+	-ish	=	_____

Here are some exceptions to the Final *E* Rule:

true + ly = truly   argue + ment = argument

nine + th = ninth   judge + ment = judgment

acknowledge + ment = acknowledgment

agree + able = agreeable

63.

The suffixes *-able* and *-ible* mean the same thing. There is no hard rule that says when each suffix should be used, so you will need to memorize the correct suffix to use with each word.

Add *-able* to the following base words:

suit _____

bend _____

honor _____

reason _____

objection_____

account _____

Add *-ible* to the base words:

contempt _____

contract _____

percept _____

collect _____

interrupt _____

resist _____

54

$64.$ When the suffixes *-ation, -ion,* or *-ly* are added, letters are often changed or dropped from the base word.

For example:

Base Word	+	Suffix	=	New Word
aviate	+	-ion	=	aviation
				(the *e* has been dropped)
exclaim	+	-ation	=	exclamation
				(the *i* has been dropped)
happy	+	-ly	=	happily
				(the *y* changed to *i*)

$65.$ Practice your suffix skills.

Hidden Suffix Search

Searching up, down, across, backward, and diagonally, find the eleven hidden suffixes in the following block of letters. Circle the suffixes as you find them. Look for: *-less, -ful, -ous, -ship, -ment, -ness, -hood, -ward, -ing, -able,* and *-ible.*

L	E	S	S	J	W
B	L	Z	Q	K	A
I	B	L	E	W	R
P	A	X	O	B	D
I	N	G	L	U	F
H	O	O	D	Q	S
S	S	E	N	L	M
Z	M	E	N	T	X

Chapter 6

Plurals: Have Some!

66. Singular means one. Plural means more than one. To form the plurals of most English nouns, add *s*. Make each of the following singular nouns plural:

Singular	Plural
1. cat	_____
2. horse	_____
3. boat	_____
4. river	_____

67. If a singular noun ends in a sound similar to the *s* sound—such as *s, x, z, ch,* or *sh*—add *es* to form the plural. Make each of the following singular nouns plural:

Singular	Plural
1. class	_____
2. fox	_____

Singular	Plural
3. waltz	_____
4. peach	_____

68. If a proper noun, such as a person's name, ends in *s*, *x*, *z*, *ch*, or *sh*, add *es* to form the plural. Make each of the following proper nouns plural:

Singular	Plural
1. Jones	_____
2. Marx	_____
3. Sanchez	_____
4. Welch	_____

69. If a noun ends in *y* preceded by a consonant, change the *y* to *i* and add *es*. For example: *diary* – *y* + *i* + *es* = *diaries*. Make each of the following singular nouns plural:

1. baby_____   5. fly _____
2. army _____   6. supply_____
3. sky_____   7. copy _____
4. quarry _____ 8. berry_____

An exception to the rule: If a proper noun ends in *y* preceded by a consonant, simply add *s* to form the plural—for example, the Purdys, the Barrys, the Henrys.

70. If a noun ends in *y* preceded by a vowel, simply add *s*. For example: *way* + *s* = *ways*. Make each of the following singular nouns plural:

1. journey _____   4. delay _____

2. chimney _____   5. alley _____

3. stay _____   6. foray _____

71. For most words that end in *f*, add *s*. For some words that end in *f* or *fe*, change the *f* or *fe* to *v* and add *es*. There is no set rule to help you remember each word, but listening to how a word is pronounced will give you a clue to how it is spelled.

For example, when you say the word *beliefs*, you hear the *fs* sound. So when you spell it you write: *belief* + *s* *(beliefs)*. When you say the word *knives*, you hear the *ves* sound. So when you spell it you write: *knife* – *fe* + *v* + *es* *(knives)*.

Practice saying the plurals for the following words. Then write each plural on the line next to the singular word.

Singular	Plural
1. thief	_____
2. chef	_____
3. giraffe	_____
4. calf	_____
5. leaf	_____
6. sheriff	_____
7. half	_____
8. cliff	_____

72. For nouns ending in *o* preceded by a consonant, add *.es.* Make each of the following singular nouns plural:

Singular	Plural
1. echo	_____
2. potato	_____
3. tomato	_____
4. veto	_____
5. torpedo	_____
6. lingo	_____

73. For musical terms that end in *o* preceded by a *.consonant,* add only *s.* Make each of the following musical terms plural:

Singular	Plural
1. alto	_____
2. banjo	_____
3. piano	_____
4. piccolo	_____
5. solo	_____
6. soprano	_____

74. Some nouns ending in *o* preceded by a consonant *.have* two plural forms. For example:

Singular:	motto	cargo	grotto	hobo
Plural 1:	mottos	cargos	grottos	hobos
Plural 2:	mottoes	cargoes	grottoes	hoboes

75. The plurals of some nouns are formed in irregular *.ways.* The spelling of the base word may change.

The spelling of both the singular and the plural may be the same. In such cases, there are no rules to follow. You just have to know the correct spelling—and you probably already do!

Show what you know! Circle the correct plural for each singular noun.

1. child:	childs	children	childes
2. foot:	feet	foots	footses
3. deer:	deers	deer	deeres
4. mouse:	mices	mouses	mice
5. man:	mans	men	many
6. tooth:	teeth	tooths	teeths

76. The English language borrows many words from Latin and Greek. Some plurals of borrowed nouns are spelled the same as they are spelled in their original language. Here are some borrowed words and their plurals:

Singular: addendum alumnus crisis thesis datum
Plural: addenda alumni crises theses data

Your dictionary is your best friend when it comes to spelling borrowed words and their plurals!

61

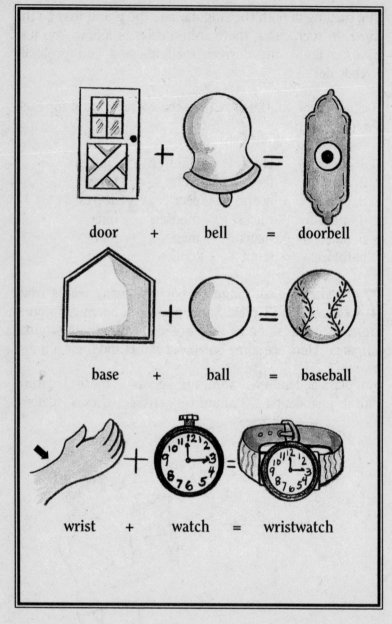

door + bell = doorbell

base + ball = baseball

wrist + watch = wristwatch

Chapter 7

Homophones and Compounds: Which Is Witch and Which Is Wristwatch?!

77. Homophones are words that sound alike but have different meanings and spellings. For example: *which* is an adjective or pronoun that refers to a particular noun, and *witch* is a hag with supernatural powers. Now you know which witch is which!

78. Because homophones sound alike, it's impossible to know how to spell a homophone unless you understand the meaning of the word. Your only clue to its correct spelling is in knowing how the word is being used.

79. Make a Definition Chart to help you remember homophone spellings.

Read the definitions of each set of homophones along with the sample sentences. Then test your skill by circling the correct homophones in the quiz.

Definition Chart

see (verb) — To detect with the eye; to recognize.
Did you *see* that great catch?
sea (noun) — A large body of salt water.
Sam and I love to swim in the *sea*.

allowed (verb, past tense) — Permitted.
The teacher *allowed* her to sharpen her pencil.
aloud (adverb) — In a voice that can be heard.
Say the word *aloud* to hear how it sounds.

ball (noun) — A three-dimensional round object.
Throw the *ball* to me!
bawl (verb) — To cry loudly.
The baby *bawled* when his mother took the bottle out of his mouth.

peace (noun) — The absence of war or conflict.
The signing of a treaty brought *peace* to the country.
piece (noun) — A part of something.
Would you like a *piece* of pizza?

---

principal (noun) — The head of a school.

Kip asked the *principal* for permission to skip gym class.

principal (adjective) — Primary, most important.

Getting an A in gym was not Kip's *principal* goal.

principle (noun) — A rule of conduct; a main fact or law.

Having high *principles* is important for elected officials.

Circle the correct homophone to complete the following sentences.

1. Which movie would you like to (see, sea)?
2. The *Titanic* hit an iceberg and sank into the (see, sea).
3. Kelly is not (allowed, aloud) to have sleepovers.
4. Reading (allowed, aloud) is a good way to share a book.
5. Emily hit the (ball, bawl) sharply and sent it flying over the fence.
6. My mother and my three aunts always (ball, bawl) when they attend weddings.
7. When the children stopped fighting, the house was at (peace, piece).
8. Give your friend a (peace, piece) of paper.
9. The office of the school (principal, principle) is on your left.
10. I have high (principals, principles), so I will not lie.
11. My (principal, principle) goal is to finish my homework early.

80. Rhyming games are also a good way to remember correct homophone spellings.

Read each sentence and circle the homophone that fits the definition.

Does the dog wag his TALE or TAIL?

Does the rain fill the PAIL or PALE?

When you listen do you HEAR or HERE?

Do you fish off the PEER or PIER?

Is one plus one TWO, TO, or TOO?

Is your homework DO, DEW, or DUE?

Are you often WRITE or RIGHT?

Do you sleep at KNIGHT or NIGHT?

Is money borrowed a LOAN or a LONE?

Do kings sit on a THRONE or a THROWN?

Is a small bug a FLEE or a FLEA?

If it's really small, is it WE or WEE?

Do you breathe HEIR or AIR?

Are clothes what you WHERE or WEAR?

When the game's over have you ONE or WON?

Are you glad you're DUN or DONE?

81. Playing with homophones is another great way to improve your skills. The following homophones have words hidden within them. Use the clues in parentheses to help you find the hidden word in each homophone. The first one is done for you.

1. The word BEAR has <u>e</u> <u>a</u> <u>r</u>. (You hear with it.)
2. The word BRAKE has ___ ___ ___ ___. (A garden tool.)
3. The word FLOWER has ___ ___ ___. (Opposite of high.)
4. The word SCENT has ___ ___ ___ ___. (A penny—and a homophone!)
5. The word BOARD has ___ ___ ___. (A rowing tool.)
6. The word BORED has ___ ___ ___. (What's found in a mine.)
7. The word KNEW has ___ ___ ___. (Not old—and a homophone!)
8. The word HEEL has ___ ___ ___. (A slippery fish.)
9. The word WHOLE has ___ ___ ___ ___. (An opening or tear—and a homophone!)
10. The word WHERE has ___ ___ ___ ___. (Not there.)

82. Show what you know in homophones. For each of the following words, write a homophone on the line provided.

1. wring _____
2. hoarse _____
3. pain _____
4. tense _____
5. sale _____

6. weak _____
7. there _____
8. colonel _____
9. hare _____
10. sun _____

83. A compound word is a word made up of two or more other words.

84. There are three types of compounds words.

• Closed compound words are written as one word:
      baseball   flashlight   homework

• Open compound words are written as separate words, but they make up a single concept:
      living room   peanut butter   fire engine

• Hyphenated compound words are written with a hyphen between the two or more words:
brand-new   well-known   twenty-one   brother-in-law

85. Closed compound words are written as one word. One word + one word = One word. For example: wrist + watch = wristwatch.

Draw a line from each word in Column 1 to the word in Column 2 that helps make a closed compound word.

Column 1
1. any   worm
   name   mate
   ship   thing
   team   plate
   earth   wreck

Column 2

Column 1	Column 2
2. flag	car
chalk	case
moon	pole
street	board
suit	light

Column 1	Column 2
3. hand	ship
space	body
foot	plant
house	writing
every	print

86. Open compound words are written as two separate words, but they make up a single concept. For example: each other.

Circle the number in front of each of the following compound words that should be written as two words.

1. sleepingbag	6. background
2. allright	7. highschool
3. whenever	8. backporch
4. nearby	9. drugstore
5. videotape	10. rightfield

87. Hyphenated compound words are written with a hyphen between two or more words. Many hyphenated compound words are adjectives, which are words that describe other words. When two or more adjectives are put together, they form a compound adjective. When a compound adjective is in front of a noun, the two describing words have a hyphen between them. For example, long-legged boy.

Long + *legged* (two words forming a compound adjective) in front of *boy* (a noun) = *long-legged boy*.

Study each one of the following hyphenated compound words. They are all written as hyphenated compounds, but some of them should not be hyphenated. Write T, for true, on the blank line if the word is correctly hyphenated. Write F, for false, if the word is incorrectly hyphenated.

____1. half-crazed lion   ____ 6. good-friend waving

____2. up-to-date news   ____ 7. old-fashioned ideas

____3. happy-girl smiles   ____ 8. pitch-dark night

____4. self-serving man   ____ 9. two-thirds majority

____5. three-days left   ____ 10. four-room house

88. If a compound noun is written as one word, form the plural by adding *s* or *es*.

For example:
Singular: schoolhouse   wristwatch   newspaper
Plural: schoolhouses   wristwatches   newspapers

89. If a compound noun is hyphenated, form the plural by making the main noun plural.

For example:
Singular: brother-in-law   passer-by   attorney-at-law
Plural: brothers-in-law passers-by   attorneys-at-law

90. Know your compound numbers! Compound numbers from twenty-one to ninety-nine are hyphenated.

For example:
ninety-nine dollars   fifty-five inches   twenty-one days

91. Simple fractions, such as one half, two thirds, and three quarters, are usually spelled without a hyphen.

For example:
I ate one half of the pie.

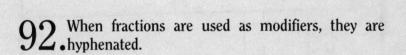

92. When fractions are used as modifiers, they are hyphenated.

For example:
He won the election by a two-thirds majority.

Chapter 8

Words, Words, and More Words!

93. Get comfortable with words. Refer to the chart on pages 73–76 to review the spellings and pronunciations of many English sounds.

How to Spell English Sounds	
Sound	Spellings
a	cat, plaid, calf, laugh
ā	maple, paid, say, freight, they, break, vein, gauge, crepe, beret
ah	farmer, ah, palm, heart, bazaar
b	belt, nibble
ch	child, patch, future, suggestion

d	**d**i**d**, a**dd**, fill**ed**
e	**e**nd, s**ai**d, **a**ny, br**ea**d, s**ay**s, pr**a**y**e**r, h**ei**fer, l**e**opard, fr**ie**nd, b**u**ry
ē	**e**qual, **ea**t, **ee**l, happ**y**, citi**e**s, c**ei**ling, k**e**y, th**e**se, mach**i**ne, p**eo**ple
ur	int**er**n, **ear**th, p**ur**ge, m**ir**th, w**or**st, jo**ur**ney
f	**f**at, du**ff**le, coug**h**, emp**h**atic
g	**g**o, e**gg**, **gu**est, ag**h**ast, fati**gue**
h	**h**erd, **wh**ole, **j**ai alai
hw	**wh**eat, **wh**ere
i	**i**t, **E**ngland, h**y**mn, b**ee**n, marr**i**age, w**o**men, b**u**sy, b**ui**ld, manag**e**
ī	**I**, **i**ce, l**ie**, sk**y**, r**ye**, **eye**, **i**sland, h**igh**, **ai**sle, h**eigh**t, b**uy**, c**o**yote, disg**ui**se
j	**j**am, **g**em, exa**gg**erate, ba**dg**er, bri**dge**, sol**d**ier, lar**ge**
k	**c**oat, **k**ind, ba**ck**, e**ch**o, a**ch**e, **q**uit, a**cc**ount, anti**que**

l	laugh, fall, kettle, epistle, tinsel
m	me, hammer, climb, column, palm
n	none, manner, knew, gnat, pneumonia
ng	long, handkerchief, harangue
o	on, watch, honor, yacht
ō	open, oak, hoe, own, comb, oh, yolk, though, bureau, sew, brooch, soul
aw	order, all, author, awful, board, bought, walk, taught, cough, Utah
oi	oil, boy
ow	scout, plow, bough, flour
p	pond, clap, snappy
r	race, carry, wrist, rhombus
s	spy, miss, celery, science, dance, tense, sword, pizza, listen
sh	shun, chenille, sure, ocean, special, suspension, mission, elation

t	time, hitting, **two**, **Th**omas, napp**ed**, de**b**t, recei**pt**, pi**zz**a
th	**th**ought, wea**th**er
u	**u**nder, **o**ven, d**ou**ble, d**oe**s, bl**oo**d
u̇	f**u**ll, w**oo**d, w**o**lf, c**ou**ld
oo	br**oo**d, r**u**le, tr**u**e, m**o**ve, fl**ew**, gr**ou**p, thr**ough**, sh**oe**, t**wo**, fr**ui**t, man**eu**ver, l**ieu**tenant
v	**v**ocal, sha**v**e, o**f**, Step**h**en
w	**w**ander, **qu**ick, **qu**iet
y	**y**ellow, bun**i**on, op**i**nion
ū	**u**nify, **u**se, barbec**ue**, b**eau**ty, **y**ew, rev**iew**, n**u**isance, vac**uu**m
z	**z**any, wa**s**, brui**s**e, ja**zz**, sci**ss**ors, **x**ylophone
zh	trea**s**ure, gara**g**e, conclu**s**ion
ə (schwa)	**a**mong, c**o**mmence, m**o**ment, **au**thority, barg**ai**n, per**i**l, caut**iou**s, circ**u**s, surg**eo**n, stud**iou**s

94.

Play with words you already know. Start by playing with your own name. Write your full name here:

_____

Study your name and answer these questions.

• Count the letters in your name.

There are _____ letters.

• Count the syllables in your first name.

There are _____ syllables.

• Look for words hiding in the letters that spell your name. Write the words below.

For example, if your name is Amanda, you will find these words hiding in your name: *A man and*

_____

_____

_____

• What other words can you spell with the letters that spell your name? For example, if your name is Amanda, you can spell these words with the letters in your name: *a, am, an, and, dam, dan, mad, man.*

_____

_____

_____

95.

One way to improve your spelling skills is to practice spelling more often. Learn to spell one new word every day. Here are challenging words from some familiar subject categories. Pick a subject and learn to spell the words that go with it.

Art
painting   museum   canvas   sculptor   sculpture   impressionist

Music
composer   lyrics   musician   piano   bass   recital

Theater
videotape   cinema   screen   film   drama   comedy

Science
chemistry   physics   atomic   formula   research   theory

Medicine
measles   health   physical   vein   thermometer   surgery

Occupations
lawyer   columnist   journalist   teacher   electrician   plumber

History
revolution   coup   military   surrender   siege   soldier

Literature
novel   parody   satire   nonfiction   preface   author

96. Type your word list. For some people, hands-on learning is easier than other methods. The act of putting your hands on each letter on a keyboard may help you remember the spelling of words.

To find out if you are a "hands-on learner," try typing the following list of words two times. First, look at the words as you type them. Second, try to type from memory.

Type: canceled   receive   Michigan   minute

97. Studying for a spelling test is sometimes easier if you study with friends than if you study alone. Turn your study time into a spelling bee. Have one person call out the words. Take turns spelling. Everyone is a winner when your test scores improve!

98. Make a Word-a-Day Calendar. Use the words in the list of 101 Commonly Misspelled Words (pages 80–81). Add words from your own spelling notebook. Write one word on each day of the month. Learn to spell one word each day until you've learned the whole list.

99. Have some spelling fun with a newspaper article. Do some or all of the following:

- Circle all the prefixes.
- Circle all the suffixes.
- Circle all the homophones.
- Circle all the compound words.
- Circle all the double consonants.
- Circle all the words hiding within words.

100. Make flash cards of words that give you trouble. Tape the cards on the walls of your room, on the bathroom mirror, on the refrigerator, and wherever else you will see them often. Study them for a few minutes every day as you go about your chores.

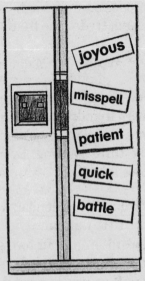

101. Learn the words on the following list of 101 Commonly Misspelled Words.

101 Commonly Misspelled Words

absence	already	believe	capital
accept	anyway	breath	capitol
achieve	arithmetic	break	career
across	awhile	brought	ceiling
address	before	business	clothes
all right	beginning	calendar	column

cough
country
dairy
deceive
dictionary
different
discipline
disease
dissatisfied
effect
eighth
eligible
eliminate
embarrass
enormous
environment
everybody
faucet
February
feud
foreign
friend
gauge
genius
gorgeous
grammar

guard
guidance
handkerchiefs
health
heart
height
hoarse
humor
illegal
iron
irrelevant
jealous
judgment
knowledge
leisure
lightning
loose
lose
marriage
mileage
minute
misspelled
muscle
neighbor
neither
ninety

ninth
noisily
occur
occasion
often
origin
parallel
piece
potatoes
quiet
quite
receive
rhyme
rhythm
seize
siege
thorough
through
tomorrow
vacuum
village
villain
voice
weird
wrestle

Answers to Puzzles and Word Games

Chapter 1: Spell Well . . . and Lots of Other Words!

5. Word-in-a-Word puzzle: hat; Bach; fat; pea; cot; mat; pot; last.

10. View: viewed; viewing; review; reviewed; preview; previewed; viewable. (These are just some of the possible answers.)

Chapter 2: Vowel Sounds: The Long and Short of It

13. Long *A* rhyming words: 1. able/table/fable; 2. afraid/braid/laid; 3. pay/day/tray; 4. lane/plane/crane. (These are just some of the possible answers.)

14. Long *E* rhyming words: 1. me/we/she; 2. weed/feed/need; 3. team/dream/gleam; 4. recede/secede/precede; 5. brief/relief/thief. (These are just some of the possible answers.)

15. *I-E* Rule—Long *E* sound: 1. believe; 2. deceit; 3. piece; 4. receive; 5. grief; 6. relief; 7. hygiene; 8. retrieve.

I-E Rule—Long *A* sound: 1. neighbor; 2. reindeer; 3. weight; 4. sleigh.

17. Long *I* rhyming words: 1. find/blind/wind; 2. shy/fly/why; 3. high/nigh/sigh; 4. shine/line/mine. (These are just some of the possible answers.)

18. Long *O* rhyming words: 1. go/no/so; 2. goat/boat/coat; 3. dough/though/although; 4. code/rode/mode. (These are just some of the possible answers.)

19. Long *U* rhyming words: 1. cue/hue/argue; 2. few/pew/yew; 3. suit/fruit/bruit; 4. tune/dune/rune; 5. moon/soon/noon. (These are just some of the possible answers.)

20. Short *a* sound: bad; factory; manners; catch.
Short *e* sound: seven; mess; dent; helmet.
Short *i* sound: fish; mint; into; picnic.
Short *o* sound: pot; locket; tongs; bother.
Short *u* sound: nut; bundle; hurry; but.

21. Short vowel sounds: 1. spaceship (short *i* in *ship*); 2. sun (short *u*); 3. band (short *a*); 4. shopkeeper (short *o* in *shop*); 5. hunt (short *u*); 6. tent (short *e*); 7. stop (short *o*); 8. cap (short *a*); 9. pitch (short *i*); 10. west (short *e*).

22. Long vowel sounds: 1. toe (long *o*); 2. tune (long *u*); 3. nine (long *i*); 4. sleet (long *e*); 5. pine (long *i*); 6. boat (long *o*); 7. team (long *e*); 8. lake (long *a*); 9. grapefruit (long *a*; long *u*); 10. ukulele (long *u*; long *e*).

Chapter 3: Consonant Sounds and Other Sounds

25. *C* sounds like an *s* or a *k*: 1. s; 2. k; 3. s; 4. k; 5. s; 6. s; 7. k; 8. s; 9. k; 10. s; 11. k; 12. s; 13. k; 14. k; 15. s; 16. k; 17. k; 18. s.

26. Spelling the *f* sound:
Philip was a frog,
Who croaked from noon to night.
The other frogs thought Philip
Was a very funny sight.

A frog named Fred called Philip
On the phone and said,
"Enough! Your croaking's giving me
An aching in my head!"

"So sorry, Fred," said Philip.
"I meant not to offend.
From now on my croaking days
Have come to a final end!"

27. Spelling the *g* sound: aghast; ghost; gown; spaghetti; guess; guard; guitar; vaguely.

29. Spelling the *j* sound: 1. T; 2. F (bridge); 3. T; 4. T; 5. F (judge); 6. T; 7. T; 8. F (pledge); 9. F (ridge); 10. T; 11. T; 12. T.

31. Spelling the *l* sound: little; kernel; long; whistle; small; kettle; legs; hill; bubbles.

32. Spelling the *n* sound: Nellie; nine; knee-high; nicest; neighborhood; Nellie; knocked; knew; gnome; gnawing; know; gnomes; Nellie; named; Noah; gnats; pneumonia.

33. Spelling the *r* sound: 1. wrong; 2. rake; 3. rain; 4. wrap; 5. wrist; 6. rap; 7. wrestling; 8. ring; 9. rhombus.

34. Spelling the *z* sound: was; please; cozy; fuzz; Xerox. (These are just some of the possible answers.)

35. Using *-ought* or *-aught*: brought; bought; haughtily; caught; thought; fought; naughty; daughter's; thoughtful; thought; caught; taught; ought; brought.

36. Spelling the *o, oo, uf, ow,* and *off* sounds: 1. enough, *uf*; 2. cough, *off*; 3. plough, *ow*; 4. though, *o*; 5. rough, *uf*; 6. bough, *ow*; 7. tough, *uf*; 8. through, *oo*.

Chapter 4: Prefixes Are Just the Beginning!

41. Base words: 1. new; 2. stop; 3. regular; 4. sane; 5. lead; 6. able; 7. continue; 8. possible; 9. literate; 10. date.

42. Adding *in-*: inadequate; indirect; inappropriate; insincere; inexpensive; indecisive.

43. Adding *im-*: impartial; impossible; impractical; immature; immobile; impatient; improbable; imprecise; immodest; immortal.

44. Adding *un-*: unhappy; unused; unhealthy; uninterested; unopened; unfair.

45. Adding *mis-*: misstate; misspell; misstep; misspend.

46. Adding *re-*: 1. rearrange; 2. reconstruct; 3. refresh; 4. recycle; 5. recapture.

47. Prefix skills: preheat; dissatisfaction; unhappy; inexpensive; improper; conform; reassign.

48. Prefix word definitions: 1. not legible; 2. not complete; 3. fill again; 4. athlete above all others.

49. Prefix test: 1. no prefix; 2. re; 3. sub; 4. no prefix; 5. re; 6. no prefix; 7. no prefix; 8. pre.

50. Hidden prefix words: 1. <u>red I al</u>ways; 2. <u>sun, lucky</u>; 3. J<u>im is in Form</u>; 4. Da<u>d is satisfied</u>; 5. <u>limp rope r</u>eached; 6. <u>in for Mal</u>lory.

Chapter 5: Suffixes Are Just the Ending!

53. Suffixes *-less* and *-ful*: 1. spotless; 2. careful; 3. childless; 4. painful; 5. friendless; 6. mindful.

54. Finding base words: 1. encourage; 2. tender; 3. happy; 4. engage; 5. soft; 6. battle.

55. Changing base words: 1. hairier; 2. sunniest; 3. lovelier; 4. decoding; 5. eroded; 6. invader; 7. thinnest; 8. tanning; 9. adorable; 10. victorious.

56. Adding *-ing*: 1. cramming; 2. gripping; 3. stabbing.
Adding *-ed*: 1. controlled; 2. admitted; 3. equipped.
Adding *-er*: 1. islander; 2. polisher; 3. customer.
Doubling consonants: 1. dropping; 2. quitter; 3. robbed; 4. maddest; 5. stoppable; 6. stepping.

60. Two-vowel base words: 1. training; 2. teacher; 3. cleanest; 4. foolish; 5. weeded; 6. fueling; 7. bearable; 8. riotous.

62. Suffixes after a final *e*: 1. caring; 2. agreement; 3. hopeful; 4. loner; 5. freedom; 6. ninety; 7. whitest; 8. purplish.

63. Suffixes *-able* and *-ible*: suitable; bendable; honorable; reasonable; objectionable; accountable; contemptible; contractible; perceptible; collectible; interruptible; resistible.

65. Hidden Suffix Search

L	E	S	S	J	W
B	L	Z	Q	K	A
I	B	L	E	W	R
P	A	X	O	B	D
I	N	G	L	U	F
H	O	O	D	Q	S
S	S	E	N	L	M
Z	M	E	N	T	X

Chapter 6: Plurals: Have Some!

66. Forming plurals: 1. cats; 2. horses; 3. boats; 4. rivers.

67. *S*-sound plurals: 1. classes; 2. foxes; 3. waltzes; 4. peaches.

68. Plural proper nouns: 1. Joneses; 2. Marxes; 3. Sanchezes; 4. Welches.

69. Change *y* to *i* and add *es*: 1. babies; 2. armies; 3. skies; 4. quarries; 5. flies; 6. supplies; 7. copies; 8. berries.

70. When a vowel precedes *y*, add *s*: 1. journeys; 2. chimneys; 3. stays; 4. delays; 5. alleys; 6. forays.

71. Words that end in *f, fe*: 1. thieves; 2. chefs; 3. giraffes; 4. calves; 5. leaves; 6. sheriffs; 7. halves; 8. cliffs.

72. Nouns ending in *o*: 1. echoes; 2. potatoes; 3. tomatoes; 4. vetoes; 5. torpedoes; 6. lingoes.

73. Musical terms ending in *o*: 1. altos; 2. banjos; 3. pianos; 4. piccolos; 5. solos; 6. sopranos.

75. Irregular plurals: 1. child/children; 2. foot/feet; 3. deer/deer; 4. mouse/mice; 5. man/men; 6. tooth/teeth.

Chapter 7: Homophones and Compounds:
Which Is Witch and Which Is Wristwatch?!

79. Circle the homophone: 1. see; 2. sea; 3. allowed; 4. aloud; 5. ball; 6. bawl; 7. peace; 8. piece; 9. principal; 10. principles; 11. principal.

80. Homophone rhyme game: tail; pail; hear; pier; two; due; right; night; loan; throne; flea; wee; air; wear; won; done.

81. Word-in-a-word: 1. ear; 2. rake; 3. low; 4. cent; 5. oar; 6. ore; 7. new; 8. eel; 9. hole; 10. here.

82. Show what you know: Here are some possible answers. 1. wring/ring; 2. hoarse/horse; 3. pain/pane; 4. tense/tents; 5. sale/sail; 6. weak/week; 7. there/their; 8. colonel/kernel; 9. hare/hair; 10. sun/son.

85. Closed compound words: 1. anything; nameplate; shipwreck; teammate; earthworm. 2. flagpole; chalkboard; moonlight; streetcar; suitcase. 3. handwriting; spaceship; footprint; houseplant; everybody.

86. Open compound words: 1. sleeping bag; 2. all right; 7. high school; 8. back porch; 10. right field

87. Hyphenated compound words: 1. T; 2. T; 3. F; 4. T; 5. F; 6. F; 7. T; 8. T; 9. T; 10. T.

My Spelling Notebook

When you find a new word you are having trouble spelling, write the word here.

_____

_____

_____

_____

_____

_____

_____

_____

_____

_____

_____

_____

_____

_____

_____

_____

_____

_____

Spelling Helpers

Know Your Numbers

one	eleven	thirty
two	twelve	forty
three	thirteen	fifty
four	fourteen	sixty
five	fifteen	seventy
six	sixteen	eighty
seven	seventeen	ninety
eight	eighteen	hundred
nine	nineteen	thousand
ten	twenty	million

Know the Days of the Week

Monday
Tuesday
Wednesday
Thursday
Friday
Saturday
Sunday

Know the Months of the Year

January
February
March
April
May
June
July
August
September
October
November
December

Know the 50 States and the Postal Service Abbreviations

AL	Alabama	NB	Nebraska
AK	Alaska	NV	Nevada
AZ	Arizona	NH	New Hampshire
AR	Arkansas	NJ	New Jersey
CA	California	NM	New Mexico
CO	Colorado	NY	New York
CT	Connecticut	NC	North Carolina
DE	Delaware	ND	North Dakota
FL	Florida	OH	Ohio
GA	Georgia	OK	Oklahoma
HI	Hawaii	OR	Oregon
ID	Idaho	PA	Pennsylvania
IL	Illinois	RI	Rhode Island
IN	Indiana	SC	South Carolina
IA	Iowa	SD	South Dakota
KS	Kansas	TN	Tennessee
KY	Kentucky	TX	Texas
LA	Louisiana	UT	Utah
ME	Maine	VT	Vermont
MD	Maryland	VA	Virginia
MA	Massachusetts	WA	Washington
MI	Michigan	WV	West Virginia
MN	Minnesota	WI	Wisconsin
MS	Mississippi	WY	Wyoming
MO	Missouri	DC	District of Columbia
MT	Montana		

Bibliography

Bell, Kathleen L., Francess Freeman Paden, and Susan Duffy Schaffrath. *McDougal, Littell English*. Evanston, IL: McDougal, Littell & Company, 1987.

Kierzek, John M., and Walker Gibson. *The Macmillan Handbook of English,* 5th Edition. New York, NY: The Macmillan Company, 1965.

Lewis, Norman. *RSVP Reading, Spelling, Vocabulary, Pronunciation*. New York: Amsco School Publications, Inc., 1967.

Wilson, Harris W., and Louis G. Locke. *The University Handbook*. New York: Holt, Rinehart and Winston, 1960.

Index